KICK-ASS QUOTES FOR MIGHTY MUMS

summersdale

MUM PWR

Text by Eve Willis

An Hachette UK Company
www.hachette.co.uk

Summersdale Publishers Ltd
Part of Octopus Publishing Group Limited
Carmelite House
50 Victoria Embankment
LONDON
EC4Y 0DZ
UK

www.summersdale.com

Printed and bound in China

ISBN: 978-1-78783-640-2

Substantial discounts on bulk quantities of Summersdale books are available to corporations, professional associations and other organizations. For details contact general enquiries: telephone: +44 (0) 1243 771107 or email: enquiries@summersdale.com.

To.............................

From.........................

AT THE END OF THE DAY MY MOST IMPORTANT TITLE IS STILL MOM-IN-CHIEF.

MICHELLE OBAMA

TO DESCRIBE
MY MOTHER WOULD
BE TO WRITE ABOUT
A HURRICANE IN ITS
PERFECT POWER.

Maya Angelou

I'M A MUM – WHAT'S YOUR SUPERPOWER?

#thismama used to have a living room. Now I just have a play room. When did that happen?

SERENA WILLIAMS

YOU KEEP SEARCHING FOR SOMEBODY AS GOOD AS YOUR MOTHER, AND THAT'S A LOSING BATTLE.

JUSTIN TIMBERLAKE

YOU CAN BE SEXY
AND STILL BE A
BADASS MOM.

KYLIE JENNER

I'M THAT MUM

Motherhood has a very humanizing effect.

MERYL STREEP

MOTHERHOOD IS THE GREATEST THING AND THE HARDEST THING.

RICKI LAKE

I GOT IT FROM MY MAMA

FELL ASLEEP WITH MY BREAST
PUMP ON AND I THINK I'M IN A
DIFFERENT DIMENSION NOW.

Chrissy Teigen

MY MOTHER IS MY ROOT, MY FOUNDATION.

MICHAEL JORDAN

I THINK IT'S LESS ABOUT PARENTING NOW FOR ME AND MORE ABOUT CROWD CONTROL.

VICTORIA BECKHAM

MUMS ARE
90%
COFFEE
AND 10%
SLEEP

NEVER, NEVER, NEVER GIVE UP. AND REMEMBER TO DANCE A LITTLE.

GLORIA STEINEM

BAD MOMENTS DON'T
MAKE BAD MOMS.

Lysa TerKeurst

MUM IS THE REAL MVP: MOST VALUABLE PARENT

Acceptance, tolerance, bravery, compassion. These are the things my mom taught me.

LADY GAGA

THERE IS NO WAY TO BE A PERFECT MOTHER AND A MILLION WAYS TO BE A GOOD ONE.

JILL CHURCHILL

LIFE DOESN'T COME WITH A MANUAL, IT COMES WITH A MOTHER.

ANONYMOUS

MUM-MAZING

Mothers always know.

OPRAH WINFREY

BECOMING A MOTHER HAS MADE ME NEXT-LEVEL CONFIDENT. I'VE NEVER FELT MORE EMPOWERED.

KELLY CLARKSON

SUPERWO*MUM*

YOU'RE STILL THE
SAME PERSON YOU
WERE BEFORE, BUT NOW
YOU'RE MORE BECAUSE
YOU'RE A MOTHER TOO.

Gwen Stefani

THERE'S NOTHING LIKE A MAMA-HUG.

TERRI GUILLEMETS

YOU NEVER KNOW WHEN
YOU'RE GONNA GET
CR*PPED ON OR WHEN
YOU'RE GONNA GET
A BIG SMILE.

BLAKE LIVELY

AIN'T NO MUMMY GOT TIME FOR THAT

FOR MOST EXHAUSTED MUMS, THEIR IDEA OF "WORKING OUT" IS A GOOD, ENERGETIC LIE-DOWN.

KATHY LETTE

IT'S NOT EASY BEING A
MOTHER. IF IT WERE EASY,
FATHERS WOULD DO IT.

Betty White

MOTHERHOOD

=

WINGING IT

My mother had a great deal of trouble with me, but I think she enjoyed it.

MARK TWAIN

MY MOTHER'S GREAT...
SHE COULD STOP YOU
FROM DOING ANYTHING,
THROUGH A CLOSED
DOOR EVEN, WITH A
SINGLE LOOK.

WHOOPI GOLDBERG

SHE'S A

COOL CHICK.

BRADLEY COOPER
ON HIS MOTHER

BORN TO MUM

If you want anything
said, ask a man; if you
want anything done,
ask a woman.

MARGARET THATCHER

I HAVE A
REALLY SWEET
DAUGHTER.
SHE WANTS
TO HUG ALL
THE OTHER
KIDS. I DIDN'T
TEACH HER
TO BE SWEET.

MILA KUNIS

9 P.M. IS THE NEW MIDNIGHT

I AM GOING TO TEACH
YOU THE RULES SO THAT
YOU'LL KNOW HOW AND
WHEN TO BREAK THEM.

Pink

I KNOW ENOUGH TO KNOW THAT WHEN YOU'RE IN A PICKLE – CALL MOM.

JENNIFER GARNER

MY MOTHER TAUGHT ME THAT THERE ARE MORE VALUABLE WAYS TO ACHIEVE BEAUTY THAN JUST THROUGH YOUR EXTERNAL FEATURES.

LUPITA NYONG'O

MAMA STYLE: SURVIVALIST

JUST BECAUSE I'M A MOTHER DOESN'T MEAN I'M NOT STILL A REBEL.

MADONNA

A MOTHER'S LOVE FOR
HER CHILD IS LIKE NOTHING
ELSE IN THE WORLD.

Agatha Christie

#COOLMUM

The natural state
of motherhood is
unselfishness.

JESSICA LANGE

SHE WAS A WONDERFUL, RARE WOMAN — YOU DO NOT KNOW; AS STRONG, AND STEADFAST, AND GENEROUS AS THE SUN.

D. H. LAWRENCE
ON HIS MOTHER

MOTHER IS A VERB. IT'S SOMETHING YOU DO. NOT JUST WHO YOU ARE.

CHERYL LACEY DONOVAN

THE
MOMAGER

That's the wonderful thing
about mothers: you can
because you must,
and you just do.

KATE WINSLET

MY FAVOURITE THING ABOUT BEING A MOM IS JUST WHAT A BETTER PERSON IT MAKES YOU ON A DAILY BASIS.

DREW BARRYMORE

LIVE, LOVE, LAUGH, CHASE LITTLE PEOPLE

I UNAPOLOGETICALLY AND
UNABASHEDLY AM DEEPLY
BIASED TOWARD MY MOTHER.

Chelsea Clinton

BEING A MOM IS THE MOST IMPORTANT JOB I HAVE.

KIM KARDASHIAN

THE PHRASE "WORKING MOTHER" IS REDUNDANT.

JANE SELLMAN

YOU SLAY, MAMA

THERE IS ONLY ONE PRETTY CHILD IN THE WORLD, AND EVERY MOTHER HAS IT.

CHINESE PROVERB

IF MEN HAD BABIES,
THEY WOULD ONLY
HAVE ONE EACH.

Diana, Princess of Wales

I LOVE

MY

TRIBE

Moms are
allowed to be sexy.
We are allowed to
still have fun.

AMBER ROSE

THE BEST THING FOR ME
HAS BEEN THROWING
ANY KIND OF PARENTING
MANUAL OUT OF
THE WINDOW.

KATE HUDSON

MY MOTHER IS A WALKING MIRACLE.

LEONARDO DICAPRIO

MUM AKA CEO OF THE FAMILY

I feel good, although
I do wake up feeling like
my grandmother.

EMILY BLUNT

AT THE END OF THE DAY, WE CAN ENDURE MUCH MORE THAN WE THINK WE CAN.

FRIDA KAHLO

"MAYBE..."

=

UNIVERSAL
MUM CODE
FOR "NO"

MOTHER IS FAR TOO CLEVER
TO UNDERSTAND ANYTHING
SHE DOES NOT LIKE.

Arnold Bennett

THINK OF STRETCH MARKS AS PREGNANCY SERVICE STRIPES.

JOYCE ARMOUR

I'M A MOTHER WITH TWO SMALL CHILDREN, SO I DON'T TAKE AS MUCH CR*P AS I USED TO.

PAMELA ANDERSON

THOU SHALT NOT TRY ME: MOOD 24:7

I LEARNED FROM HER HOW COMPLICATED AND WONDERFUL WE WOMEN CAN BE.

PENÉLOPE CRUZ ON HER MOTHER

NOTHING ELSE EVER
WILL EVER MAKE YOU
AS HAPPY OR AS SAD,
AS PROUD OR AS TIRED.

Elia Parsons
on motherhood

QUEEN OF
MAYHEM

Sometimes
you gotta be a
beauty and
a beast.

NICKI MINAJ

MOST MOTHERS ARE INSTINCTIVE PHILOSOPHERS.

HARRIET BEECHER STOWE

ALL MOTHERLY LOVE IS REALLY WITHOUT REASON AND LOGIC.

JOAN CHEN

MUM IN
A MILLION

I'm always like, "What would mommy do?"

WILLOW SMITH

I CAME TO REALIZE OVER TIME THAT MY MOM WAS THE HERO.

TREVOR NOAH

MUMSTER:
WHAT
HAPPENS TO
MUM AFTER
SHE COUNTS
TO THREE

THERE'S NOTHING A MAN
CAN DO, THAT I CAN'T DO
BETTER AND IN HEELS.

Ginger Rogers

I FEEL A LOT MORE LIKE A WOMAN. MORE FEMININE, MORE SENSUAL. AND NO SHAME.

BEYONCÉ ON BECOMING A MOTHER

A QUEEN, A WARRIOR,
A WOMAN, A LEADER,
A REBEL; MY MOTHER.

ALICIA KEYS

AIN'T NO 'HOOD LIKE MOTHERHOOD

A MAN DOES WHAT HE CAN; A WOMAN DOES WHAT A MAN CANNOT.

ISABEL ALLENDE

SHE TAUGHT ME THAT FEAR
IS NOT AN OPTION.

Diane von Fürstenberg

I DON'T WANT TO SLEEP LIKE A BABY; I WANT TO SLEEP LIKE MY HUSBAND

A woman is like a
tea bag – you never know
how strong she is until
she gets in hot water.

ANONYMOUS

MY MOTHER DESPERATELY TRIED TO TELL ME... DON'T BE ASHAMED.

EMMA WATSON

NO ONE'S REALLY DOING IT PERFECTLY.

REESE WITHERSPOON
ON RAISING CHILDREN

TOUGH MOTHER

Biology is the
least of what makes
someone a mother.

OPRAH WINFREY

YOU ARE BRAVER THAN YOU BELIEVE, STRONGER THAN YOU SEEM, AND SMARTER THAN YOU THINK.

A. A. MILNE

MAMA
MANTRA:
THEY'LL BE
ASLEEP SOON

YOU HAVE WHAT IT TAKES
TO BE A VICTORIOUS,
INDEPENDENT,
FEARLESS WOMAN.

Tyra Banks

SOONER OR LATER WE ALL QUOTE OUR MOTHERS.

BERN WILLIAMS

I WANT MY CHILDREN
TO HAVE ALL THE THINGS
I COULDN'T AFFORD.
THEN I WANT TO MOVE
IN WITH THEM.

PHYLLIS DILLER

I RUN ON CAFFEINE AND KISSES

SOMETIMES THE STRENGTH OF MOTHERHOOD IS GREATER THAN NATURAL LAWS.

BARBARA KINGSOLVER

ANY MOTHER COULD
PERFORM THE JOBS OF
SEVERAL AIR TRAFFIC
CONTROLLERS WITH EASE.

Lisa Alther

SILENCE IS GOLDEN. UNLESS YOU HAVE KIDS, THEN SILENCE IS JUST PLAIN SUSPICIOUS.

She was indispensable
to high generation, hated
at tea parties, feared in
shops, and loved at crises.

THOMAS HARDY ON HIS MOTHER

I THINK IT'S REALLY IMPORTANT FOR EVERY MOTHER TO FIND THEIR OWN WAY.

SOLANGE

THE BEST PART IS THAT YOU ARE MY MUM.

KELLY OSBOURNE

MOTHERS ARE MAGICAL

Mothers are all
slightly insane.

J. D. SALINGER

ALL WOMEN BECOME LIKE THEIR MOTHERS. THAT IS THEIR TRAGEDY. NO MAN DOES. THAT IS HIS.

OSCAR WILDE

JUST

ANOTHER

MANIC

MUM-DAY

WE'RE ALWAYS BLUFFING,
PRETENDING WE KNOW BEST,
WHEN MOST OF THE TIME
WE'RE JUST PRAYING WE
WON'T SCREW UP TOO BADLY.

Jodi Picoult on parenting

MOTHERHOOD WAS THE GREAT EQUALIZER FOR ME.

ANNIE LENNOX

I WONDER, "HOW ON EARTH DOES ANYBODY DO THIS ALONE?" I HAVE THE UTMOST RESPECT FOR MOTHERS AND SINGLE MOTHERS.

CHRISSY TEIGEN

SHE IS FEARLESS, BRAVE AND BOLD

THE ONE THING YOU'VE GOT TO BE PREPARED TO DO AS A PARENT IS NOT TO BE LIKED FROM TIME TO TIME.

EMMA THOMPSON

THERE IS NO LIMIT TO
WHAT WE, AS WOMEN,
CAN ACCOMPLISH.

Michelle Obama

I'M THE MUM THEY WARNED YOU ABOUT

You gotta
watch out for
the moms.

ZAC EFRON

WE HAVE A SECRET
IN OUR CULTURE, AND
IT'S NOT THAT BIRTH
IS PAINFUL. IT'S THAT
WOMEN ARE STRONG.

LAURA STAVOE HARM

MOTHERHOOD IS JUST ABOUT INSTINCT.

KOURTNEY KARDASHIAN

I RUN
THINGS

What is best
in me I owe to her.

BARACK OBAMA

NOTHING CAN REALLY PREPARE YOU FOR THE SHEER OVERWHELMING EXPERIENCE OF WHAT IT MEANS TO BECOME A MOTHER.

CATHERINE, DUCHESS OF CAMBRIDGE

MAY YOUR COFFEE BE STRONGER THAN YOUR TODDLER

IF I CAN KEEP ONE
ALIVE, I'LL BE REALLY
PROUD OF MYSELF.

Olivia Wilde on motherhood

ALL THAT I AM, OR HOPE TO BE, I OWE TO MY ANGEL MOTHER.

ABRAHAM LINCOLN

NOTHING IS EVER WHAT YOU THINK IT'S GOING TO BE AT ALL.

DAWN FRENCH

CHAOS
COMMANDER

SLEEP AT THIS POINT IS JUST A CONCEPT, SOMETHING I'M LOOKING FORWARD TO INVESTIGATING IN THE FUTURE.

AMY POEHLER

WE ARE BORN FROM LOVE;
LOVE WAS OUR MOTHER.

Rumi

YOU CAN'T SCARE ME – I HAVE KIDS

"

Don't tell your kids
you had an easy
birth or they won't
respect you.

JOAN RIVERS

MY MOM SAID THE ONLY REASON MEN ARE ALIVE IS FOR LAWN CARE AND VEHICLE MAINTENANCE.

TIM ALLEN

USUALLY THE TRIUMPH OF MY DAY IS, YOU KNOW, EVERYBODY MAKING IT TO THE POTTY.

JULIA ROBERTS

HUSTLE
AND
HEART

As women and as moms
we try to do it all but
it sure ain't easy.

BROOKLYN DECKER

WHATEVER ELSE IS UNSURE IN THIS STINKING DUNGHILL OF A WORLD A MOTHER'S LOVE IS NOT.

JAMES JOYCE

ALEXA, FEED MY KIDS

MOTHERHOOD IS LEARNING
ABOUT THE STRENGTHS YOU
DIDN'T KNOW YOU HAD, AND
DEALING WITH THE FEARS
YOU NEVER KNEW EXISTED.

Linda Wooten

CHILDREN ARE LIKE CRAZY, DRUNKEN SMALL PEOPLE IN YOUR HOUSE.

JULIE BOWEN

YOU WANT TO TORTURE SOMEONE? HAND THEM AN ADORABLE BABY THEY LOVE WHO DOESN'T SLEEP.

SHONDA RHIMES

RUNNING LATE IS MY CARDIO

OF ALL THE RIGHTS OF WOMEN, THE GREATEST IS TO BE A MOTHER.

LIN YUTANG

THE MAJORITY OF MY DIET IS
MADE UP OF THE FOODS THAT
MY KID DIDN'T FINISH.

Carrie Underwood

MY SQUAD
CALLS ME
MAMA

Motherhood is the biggest gamble in the world. It is the glorious life force. It's huge and scary — it's an act of infinite optimism.

GILDA RADNER

I CAN BE COVERED IN SPIT-UP ON A CONFERENCE CALL WHILE I'M PUMPING AND THAT'S OK, BECAUSE THIS IS MY PERFECT.

KERRY WASHINGTON

IT'S ABOUT JUST GETTING THEM TO LAUGH RATHER THAN GETTING IN POWER STRUGGLES.

MARCIA CROSS

MUM LIFE IS THE BEST LIFE

A smart mother often makes a better diagnosis than a poor doctor.

AUGUST BIER

I THINK MY LIFE BEGAN WITH WAKING UP AND LOVING MY MOTHER'S FACE.

GEORGE ELIOT

JUST A
MUM BOSS,
BUILDING
HER EMPIRE

YOU CAN BE A MOTHER
AND STILL BE
COMPLETELY SEXY.

Fergie

WHEN I'M TIRED, I REST. I SAY, "I CAN'T BE A SUPERWOMAN TODAY."

JADA PINKETT SMITH

BECOMING A MOM TO ME
MEANS THAT YOU HAVE
ACCEPTED THAT FOR THE
NEXT 16 YEARS OF YOUR
LIFE, YOU WILL HAVE
A STICKY PURSE.

NIA VARDALOS

IF YOU ARE A MOM,
YOU ARE A SUPERHERO.
PERIOD.

Rosie Pope

I'VE LEARNED SOMETHING ABOUT KIDS – THEY DON'T DO WHAT YOU SAY; THEY DO WHAT YOU DO.

JENNIFER LOPEZ

MUM
PWR!

If you're interested in finding out more about our books, find us on Facebook at **Summersdale Publishers** and follow us on Twitter at **@Summersdale**

www.summersdale.com